WASHINGTON, D.C.

GERALD & MARC
HOBERMAN

WASHINGTON, D.C.

GERALD & MARC
HOBERMAN

Photographs in celebration of the nation's city

Text by Beverley Brackett

UNA PRESS, INC.
in association with
THE GERALD & MARC HOBERMAN COLLECTION
CAPE TOWN • LONDON • NEW YORK

Photography and production control: Gerald & Marc Hoberman
Design: Gerald Hoberman, Marc Hoberman, Roelien Theron
Digital scanning and reproduction: Marc Hoberman
Text: Beverley Brackett
Cartography: Peter Slingsby

Mighty Marvelous Little Books are published for Una Press, Inc. by
The Gerald & Marc Hoberman Collection
PO Box 60044, Victoria Junction, 8005, Cape Town, South Africa
Telephone: 27-21-419 6657 Fax: 27-21-418 5987 e-mail: office@hobermancollection.com
www.hobermancollection.com

International marketing, picture library, and corporate sales
Una Press, Inc./Hoberman Collection (USA), Inc. representing
The Gerald & Marc Hoberman Collection
PO Box 880206, Boca Raton, FL 33488, USA
Telephone: (561) 542 1141 e-mail: hobcolus@bellsouth.net

ISBN 10 : 1–919734–77–5
ISBN 13 : 9781919734-77-4

First published 2003, Reprinted 2007

Printed in Singapore

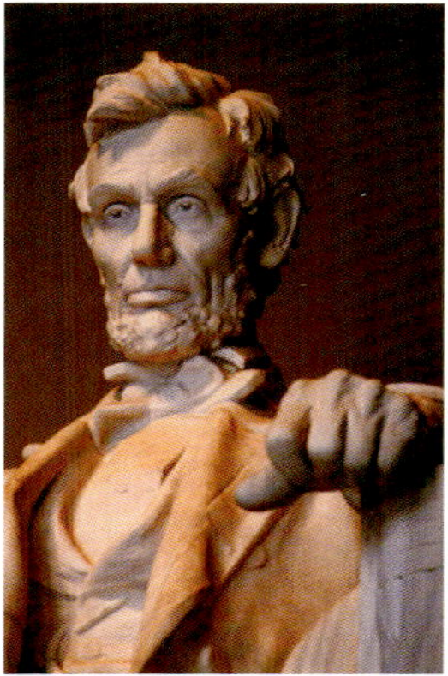

ABRAHAM LINCOLN

CONTENTS

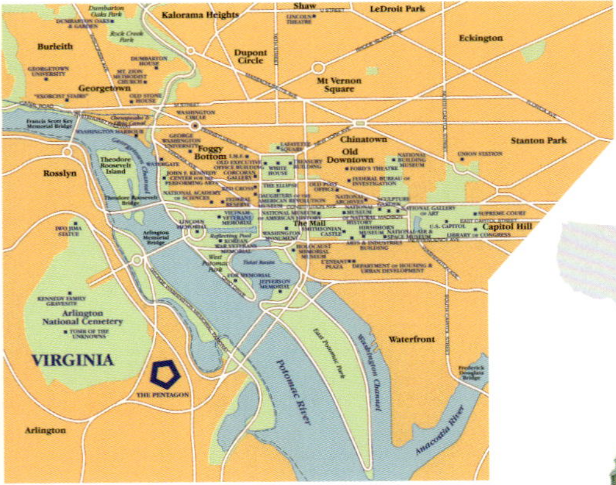

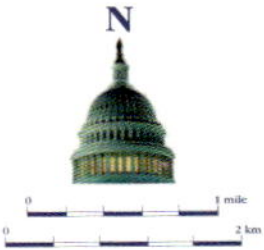

WASHINGTON, D.C.

Introduction

Washington, D.C. at the awakening of spring is a celebration of life itself. Crowds of people in a festive mood enjoy a magical time as they delight in the profusion of delicate cherry blossoms shimmering in the late afternoon sunshine. Joy and laughter are in the air.

Elsewhere, airplanes land at and take off from the Ronald Reagan Washington National Airport. Occasionally a convoy of presidential helicopters whirls overhead. Yet only a short distance away is tranquil Roosevelt Island – a wildlife sanctuary in the Potomac River.

D.C., as it is affectionately known, is monumental and inspirational, reminiscent of classical Greece and Rome – the ancient cradle of democracy. Its wide streets lead to some of the most important headquarters in the nation. The White House, official residence of the United States President, is arguably the most influential office in the world!

The city is a cultural treasure house. Its superb museums and galleries – repositories of national treasures such as the original Constitution of the United States – attract millions of visitors each year.

Arlington National Cemetery, the final resting place of heroes, presidents, leaders, and soldiers of valor, is where the Kennedys are buried. The Tomb of the Unknowns is guarded around the clock by an impressive ceremonial honor guard. Nearby stands the Pentagon, headquarters of the Department of Defense.

Then there are the neighborhoods: elegant Embassy Row; urban, hip and trendy Georgetown; and ethnically diverse Adams Morgan, among others.

We are delighted and privileged to share with you the best of the nation's capital as we see it.

Gerald Hoberman M Hoberman

GERALD & MARC HOBERMAN
Washington D.C.

THE METRORAIL

In the years since its opening in 1976, the Washington, D.C. Metrorail system, or "Metro" as it is known, has grown by leaps and bounds, and its distinctive subway trains now carry almost 600,000 passengers a day. Spread across five subway lines, Metrorail's eighty-three stations – including the famous Foggy Bottom-GWU station seen here – funnel workers, residents and tourists from the suburbs of Maryland and Virginia right into the heart of Washington, D.C.

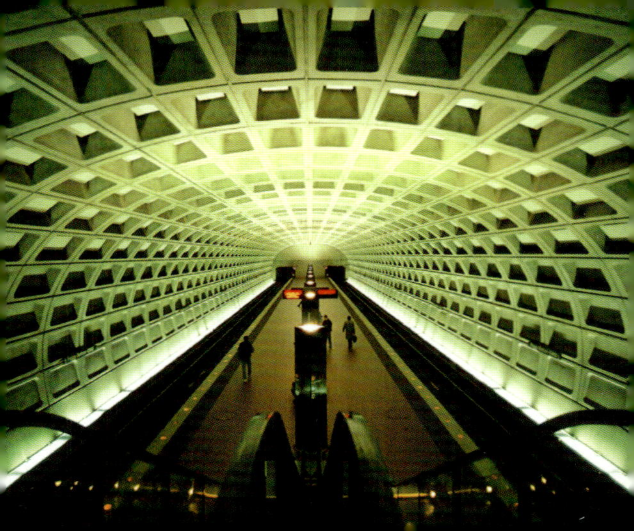

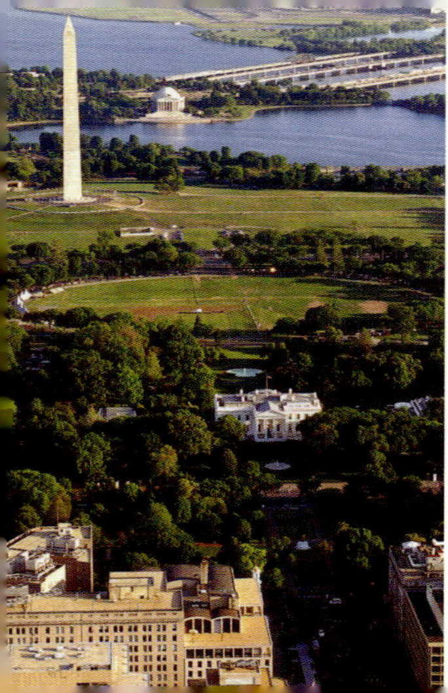

Left *In 1846 Virginia petitioned to have its portion of the District of Columbia – the city of Alexandria and part of Fairfax county – returned. Congress agreed to the request, leaving Washington, D.C. with its present-day boundaries.*

Right *Spring along the Tidal Basin.*

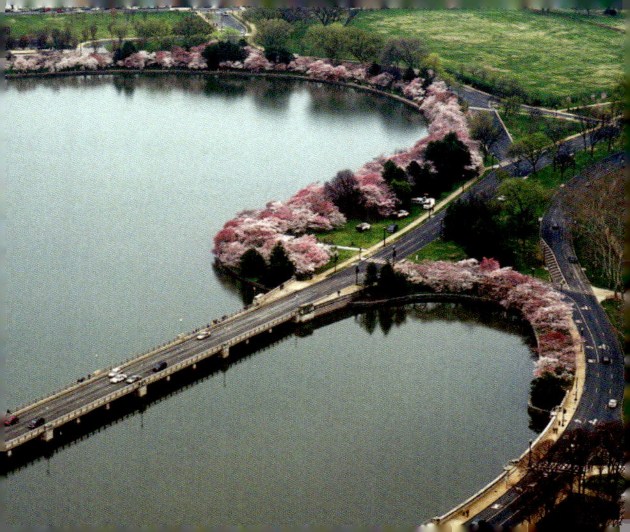

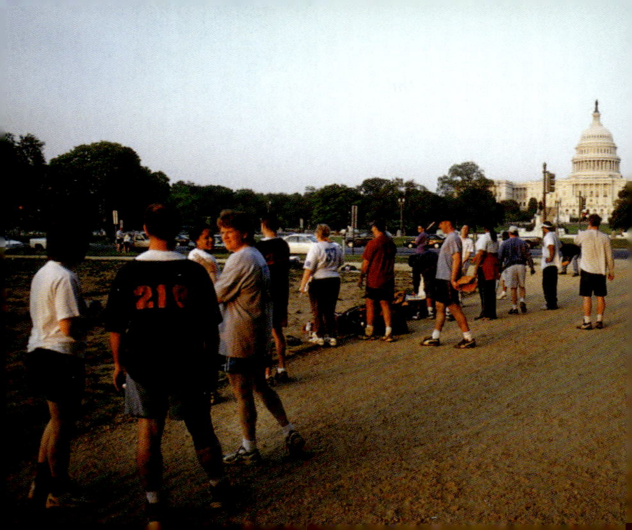

Left *Summertime in the capital.*

Right *One of the most recognizable monuments in the world, the 555-foot tall Washington Monument towers over the Washington, D.C. landscape. Visitors who take the opportunity to ride the elevator to the top of the monument are treated to an unrivaled panoramic view.*

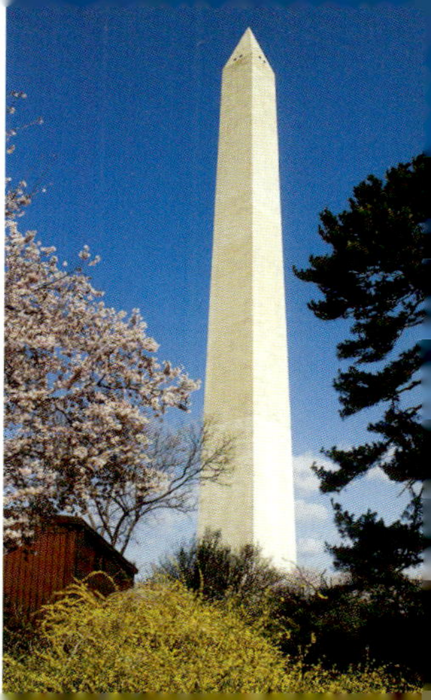

The White House

The address of the most famous residence in the United States is 1600 Pennsylvania Avenue NW. For much of its existence, the White House was known as either the President's House or the Executive Mansion. In 1901 President Theodore Roosevelt changed its name to the White House, thereby officially acknowledging the building's nickname, derived from the coats of whitewash applied to the exterior.

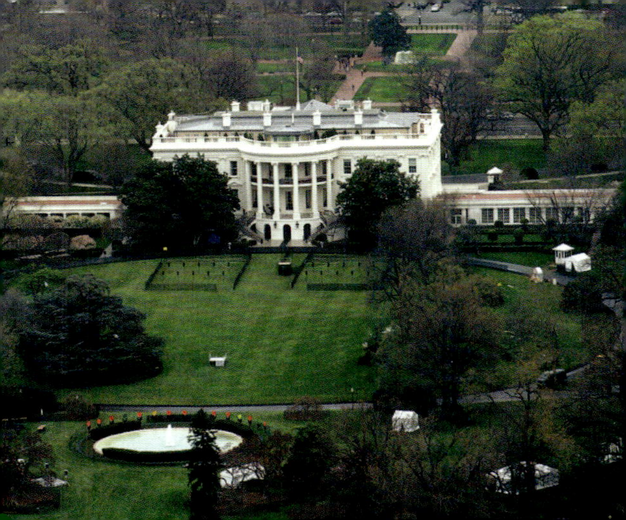

WHITE HOUSE WILDLIFE

The grey squirrels that live in the trees of the White House are carrying on a tradition that dates back to the earliest days of the presidency. During its long and distinguished service as the "People's House," the White House has often served as home to a wide variety of wild animals, many of them presidential pets. Thomas Jefferson owned a mockingbird named Dick and kept caged bears on the White House lawn. John Quincy Adams kept a pet alligator and Martin van Buren had two pet tiger cubs.

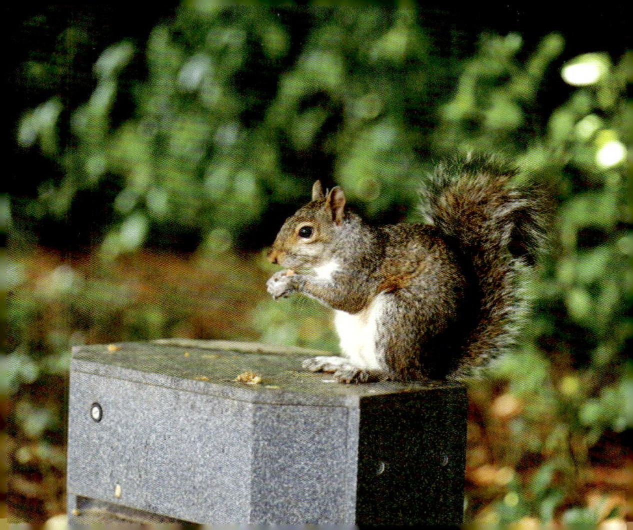

The Diplomatic Side of the Capital

The capital was disdained by foreign diplomats for its provincialism and lack of amenities. The summer heat and humidity were considered so unpleasant that British diplomats assigned to Washington, D.C. received hardship pay. With the advent of air-conditioning, and a bustling cultural life, the nation's capital evolved into what is today widely considered a plum posting. Many nations, including (clockwise from top left) Indonesia, The People's Republic of China, Turkey, and Luxembourg have purchased elegant buildings to house their delegations.

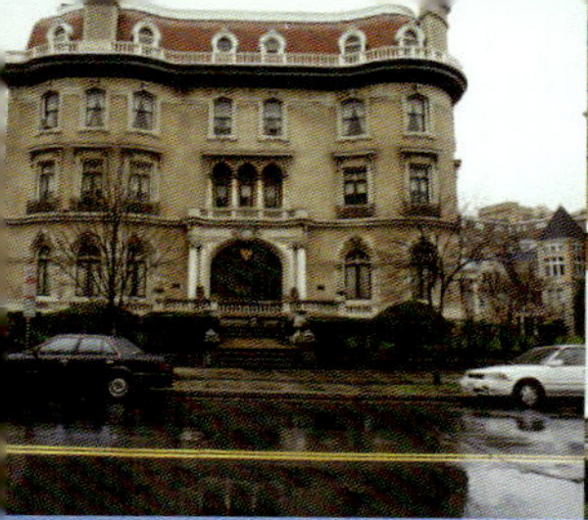
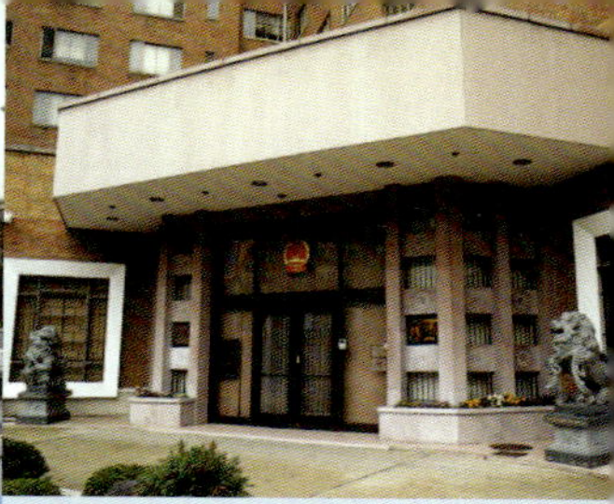
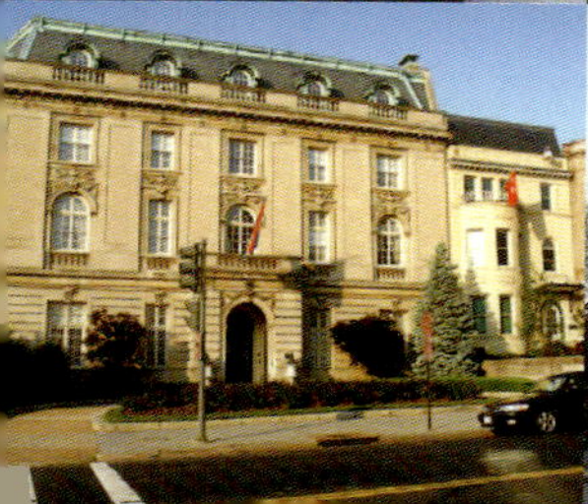
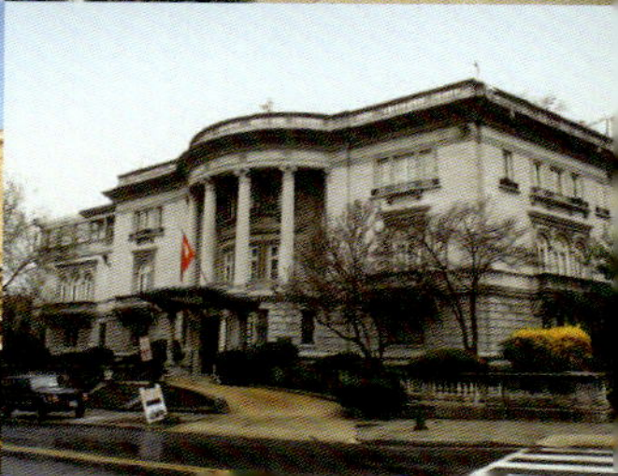

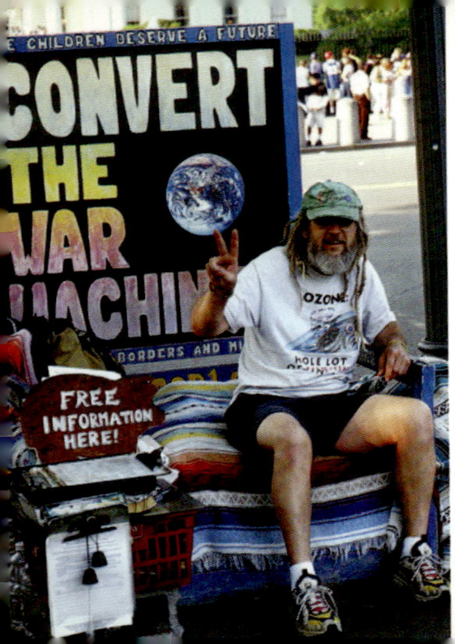

Left *Its location directly across the street from the White House makes Lafayette Square the perfect site for protestors and demonstrators of all types and political persuasions.*
Right *Fourth of July celebration.*

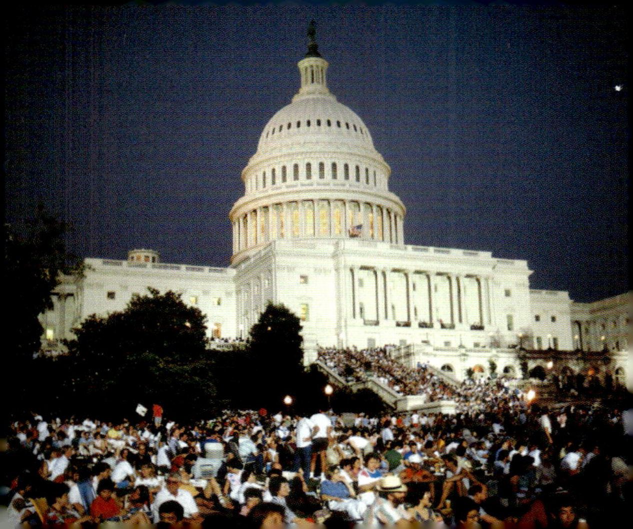

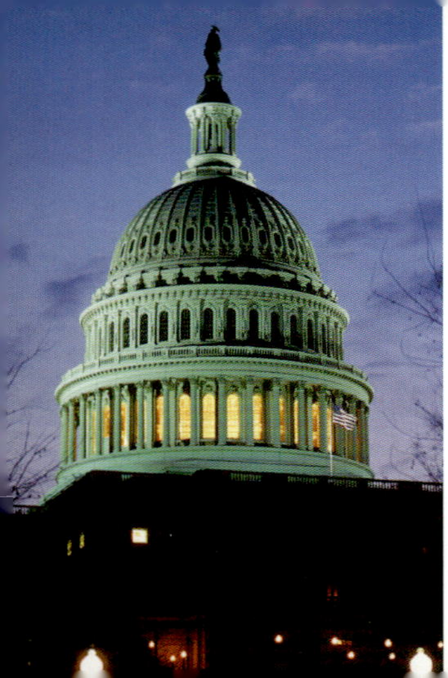

Capitol Dome *In an age when wonders of architecture are so commonplace that city dwellers and suburbanites alike take them for granted, the Capitol dome still impresses with its size and dignity. A marvel of engineering, the dome weighs almost nine million pounds.*

***Freedom*, Capitol Dome** *Thomas Crawford's seven-ton bronze statue,* Freedom, *gazes eastward over Capitol Hill from her perch atop the United States Capitol dome. In the one hand she holds a sword, and in the other, a shield and wreath.*

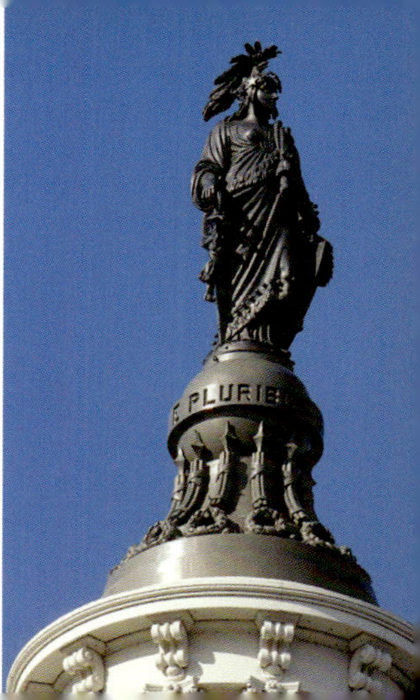

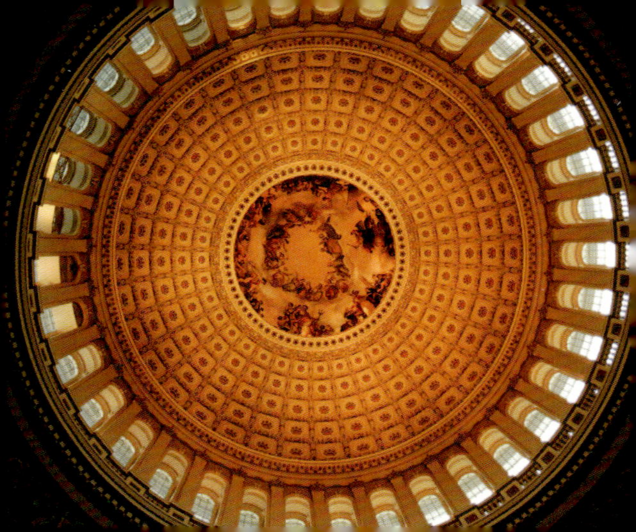

Left *Rotunda, United States Capitol.*
Right *Adelaide Johnson's sculpture, housed in the Rotunda, depicts the famous suffragettes, Lucretia Mott, Elizabeth Cady Stanton, and Susan B. Anthony. Lucretia Mott was a Quaker minister famed for her tart tongue and no-nonsense demeanor.*

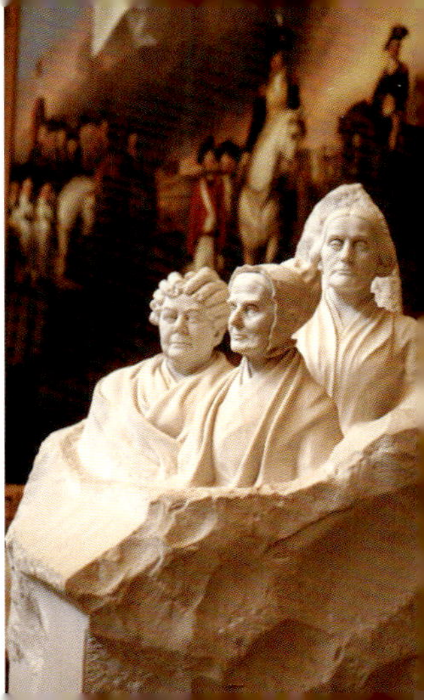

Minerva Bestows Knowledge

The United States Capitol dome's great fresco, *The Apotheosis of Washington*, depicts a number of prominent Americans interacting with figures from classical mythology. Minerva, the Roman goddess of wisdom and patroness of the arts and trades, points to an electric generator that creates power stored in batteries. At the same time she seems to offer guidance to Benjamin Franklin, inventor and statesman; Samuel Morse, inventor of the telegraph; and Robert Fulton, creator of the first commercially viable steamboat.

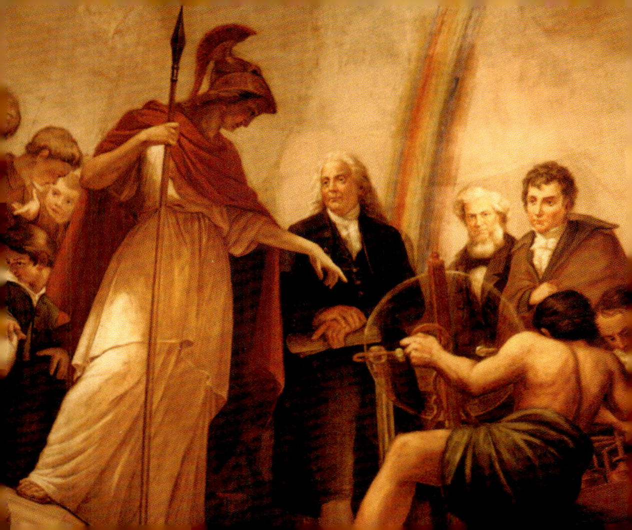

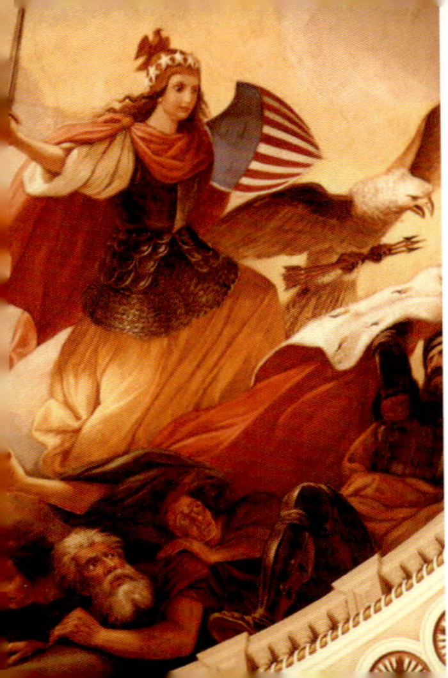

Left *The group of figures known as "War" in Italian artist Constantino Brumidi's stunning fresco,* The Apotheosis of Washington, *includes this representation of Armored Freedom.*
Right *The Old Senate Chamber once resounded with the speeches of some of America's most eloquent senators.*

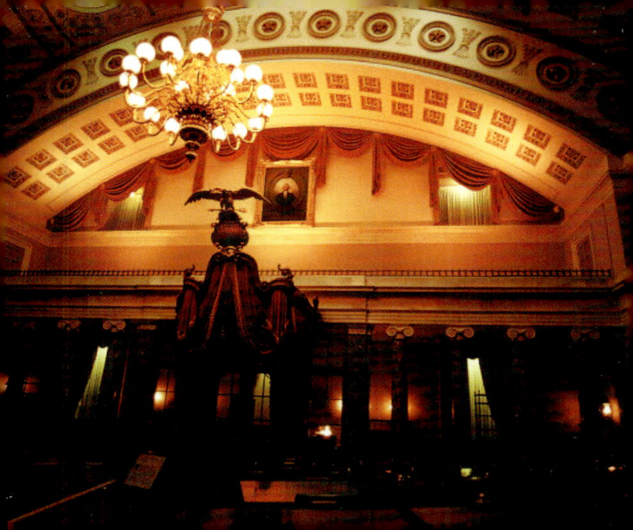

Supreme Court of the United States

Since 1935, the Chief Justice and eight Associate Justices of the Supreme Court have heard oral arguments and issued opinions from this imposing Greek Revival-style building. Those entering the Supreme Court pass under a lintel carved with the famous motto "Equal Justice Under Law." This guiding principle of American jurisprudence requires that all those appearing in the country's courts receive a fair hearing, irrespective of the economic or social status of the parties involved.

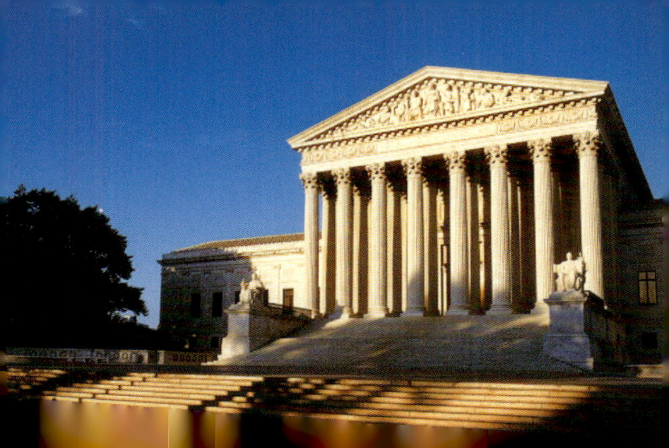

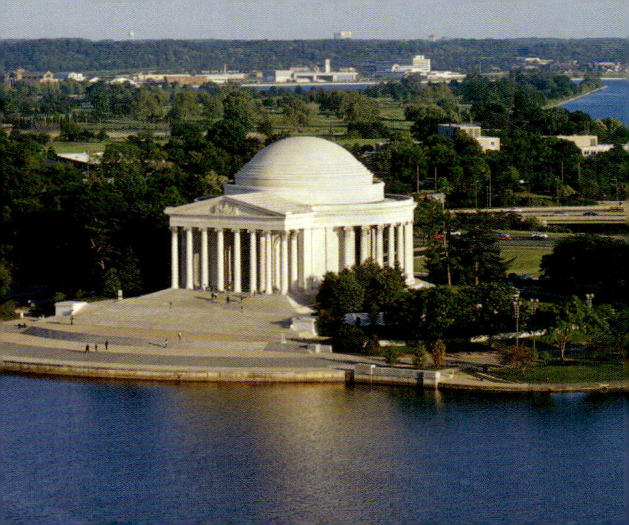

A Tribute to Thomas Jefferson

Styled after the Pantheon in Rome, the Jefferson Memorial was designed by John Russel Pope, who was also the architect of two other Washington, D.C. landmarks, the United States National Archives Building and the National Gallery of Art. Pope's design served as both a homage to and a reflection of Jefferson's aesthetic preferences.

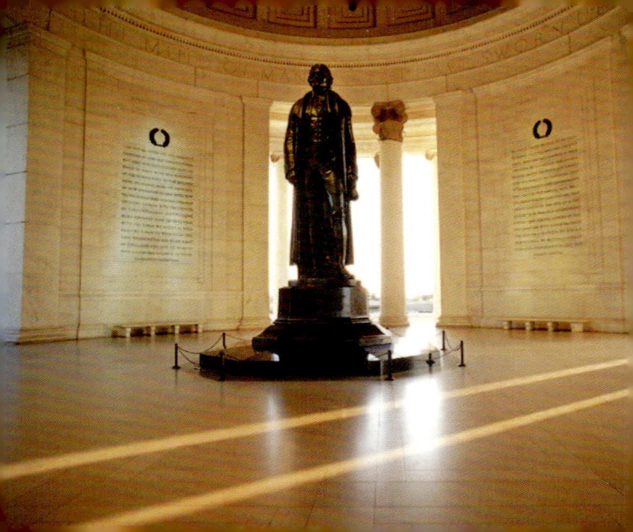

Statue of Thomas Jefferson

The ideals of Thomas Jefferson, president of the United States between 1801 and 1809, were perhaps the most influential factors in shaping the American nation at its birth. His firm belief that Americans were capable of governing themselves led to the establishment of a democratic government that has flourished for over 200 years and continues to defend and expand on human freedoms. Visitors to the colonnaded Jefferson Memorial are greeted by a majestic nineteen-foot bronze statue of the former president created by Rudolph Evans.

The Three Servicemen, Vietnam Veterans Memorial

Frederick Hart's life-sized sculpture of three young soldiers, dressed for combat, forms part of the Vietnam Veterans Memorial. The bronze statue, added to the memorial in late 1984, depicts both the camaraderie of these men and their essential aloneness, and shows the ethnic diversity and youthfulness of the soldiers who fought in the Vietnam War, the longest war in which Americans fought.

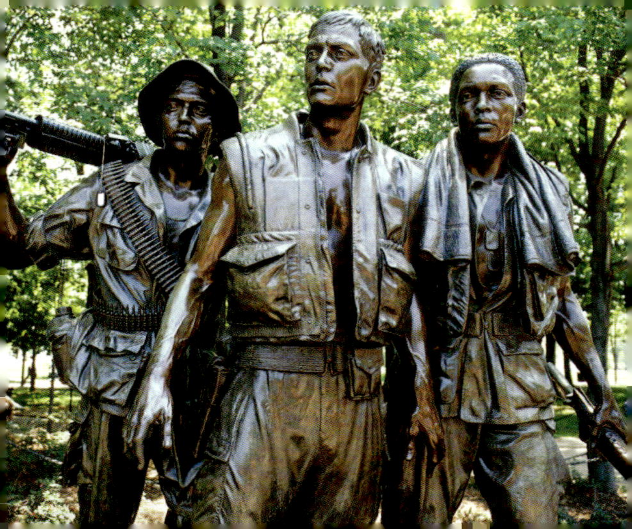

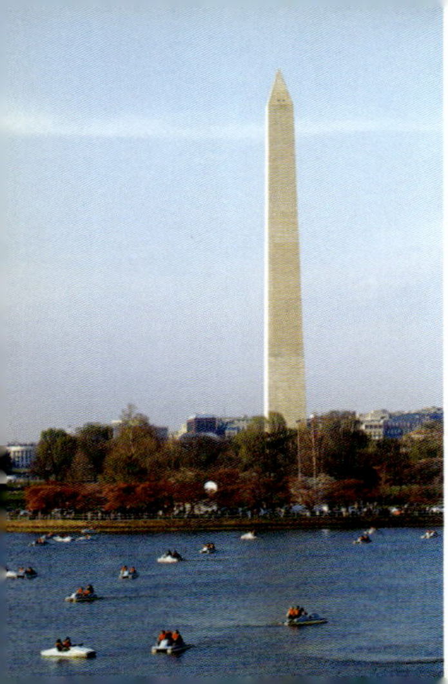

Left *The Washington Monument.*
Right *Working mainly from photographs, sculptor Daniel Chester French labored for thirteen years with the Piccirilli brothers to carve twenty-eight identical blocks of Georgia marble into the seated, pensive figure of Abraham Lincoln in the center of the Lincoln Memorial.*

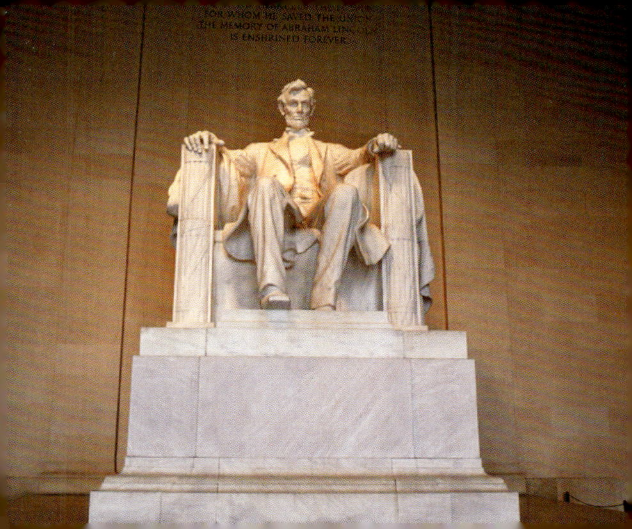
FOR WHOM HE SAVED THE UNION
THE MEMORY OF ABRAHAM LINCOLN
IS ENSHRINED FOREVER

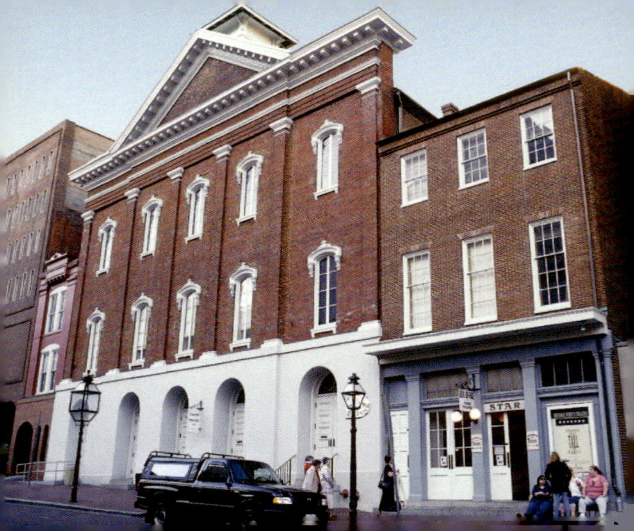
STAR

Ford's Theatre

In a city where history-making events seem to take place on every street corner, Ford's Theatre is of special significance. Here, on April 14, 1865, President Abraham Lincoln was assassinated while watching a performance. His killer was John Wilkes Booth, an actor and Southern sympathizer.

UNION STATION

Beautifully restored in 1988 at a cost of $160 million, Union Station now brims with life and activity as visitors come to shop, dine, go to the movies, and even catch a train. Built to consolidate railroad traffic in the nation's capital, the Beaux Arts-style building was designed by Daniel H. Burnham. Its main archways were inspired by the Arch of Constantine in Rome. In the years following its opening in 1907, Union Station, once the largest station in the world, served as the arrival point for presidents, world leaders, and celebrities.

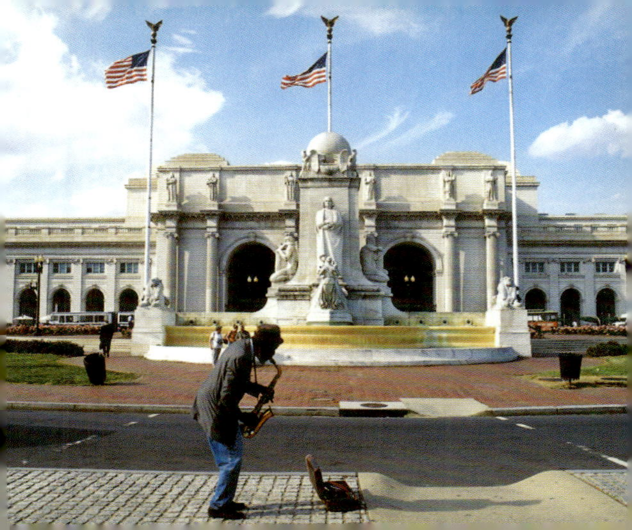

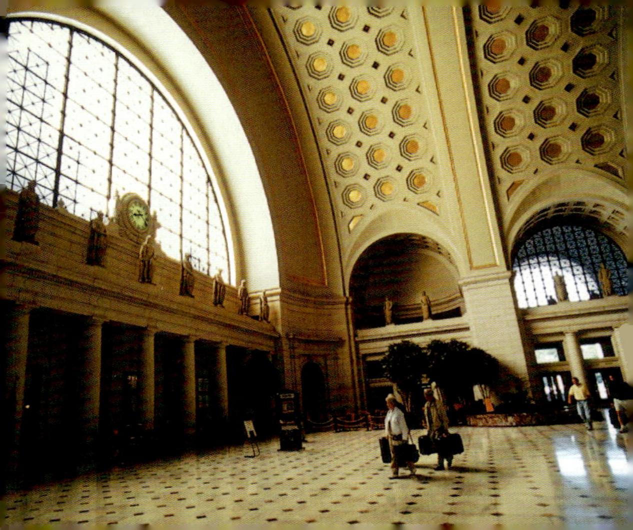

Main Hall, Union Station

To step into the restored Main Hall of Union Station is to return to an era when train travel was a glorious and elegant adventure. The hall was modeled after Rome's Baths of Diocletian and its barrel-vaulted ceiling is covered with seventy pounds of twenty-two-carat gold leaf, creating an aura of sumptuousness and majesty. Visitors will notice a series of thirty-six plaster statues of Roman Legionnaires, created by Louis Saint-Gaudens, arrayed around the balcony, .

Chinatown's Friendship Archway

A gift from Washington, D.C.'s "sister city," Beijing, this massive, ornately carved gateway over H Street is the world's largest single-span Chinese archway. Designer Alfred Liu used the traditional *duo gong* carved wood system, which does not permit the use of nails or any other metal connectors. Standing forty-seven feet high and sixty-one feet wide, the arch features seven roofs weighing a total of sixty-three tons, and is decorated with a wide variety of intricately carved animals, including fanciful Chinese dragons.

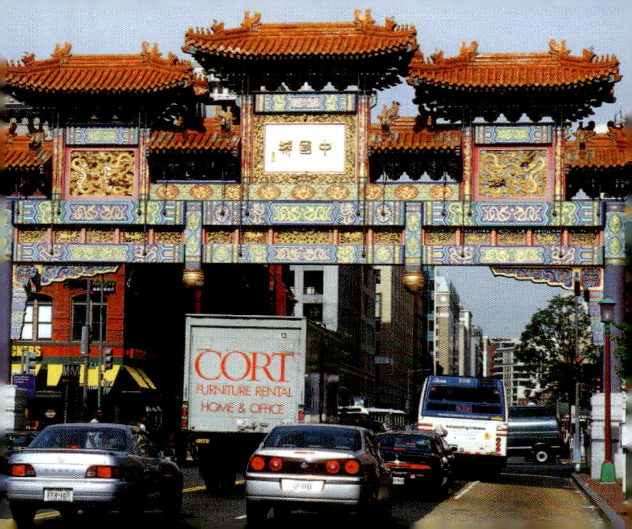
中國城
CORT
FURNITURE RENTAL
HOME & OFFICE

FEDERAL BUREAU OF INVESTIGATION

The world-renowned Federal Bureau of Investigation was established in 1908 as an arm of the Department of Justice to investigate violations of federal criminal law. Since then, the Bureau's mission has grown to include protecting the United States from foreign espionage and terrorist activities. The F.B.I.'s national headquarters in Washington, D.C. is named after its most famous and longest serving director, J. Edgar Hoover.

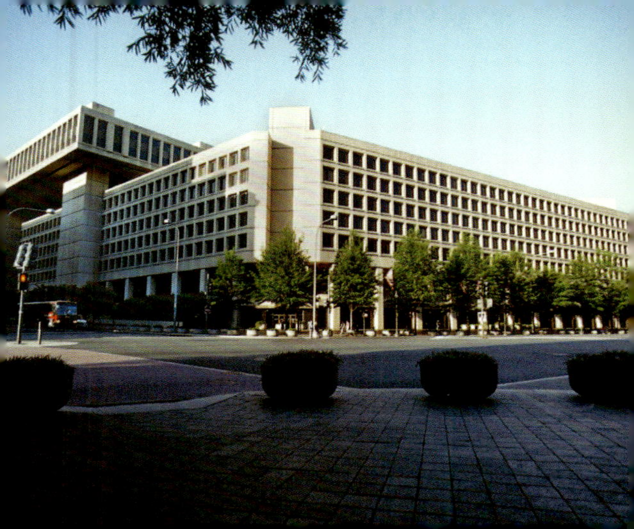

John F. Kennedy Center for the Performing Arts

Although Congress authorized the creation of a cultural center for Washington, D.C. in 1958, construction only began after the assassination of President John F. Kennedy in 1963. Designated a memorial to the young president, who had been a champion of the arts, the Kennedy Center opened to the public on September 8, 1971 with a performance of Leonard Bernstein's *Mass* at the Opera House. Since then, it has become one of the city's most prominent cultural institutions.

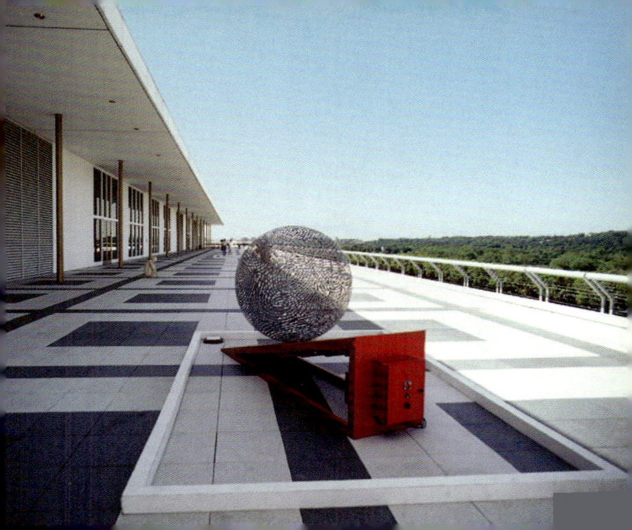

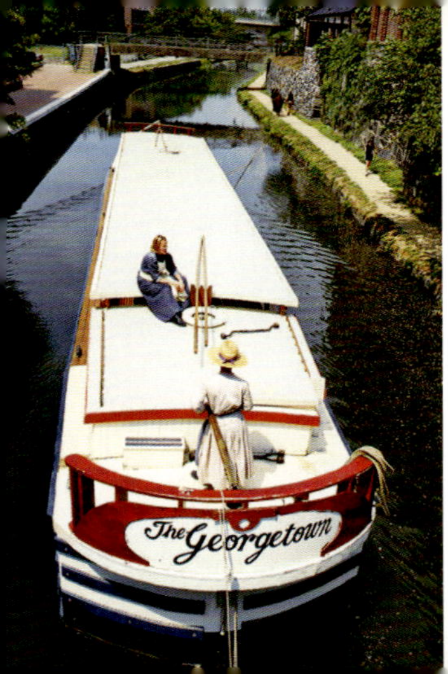

Left *The towpath alongside the Chesapeake and Ohio Canal in Georgetown is often packed with locals and tourists out to enjoy a stroll in the shade of the trees that line the banks.*
Right *Sculpture of Albert Einstein, National Academy of Sciences.*

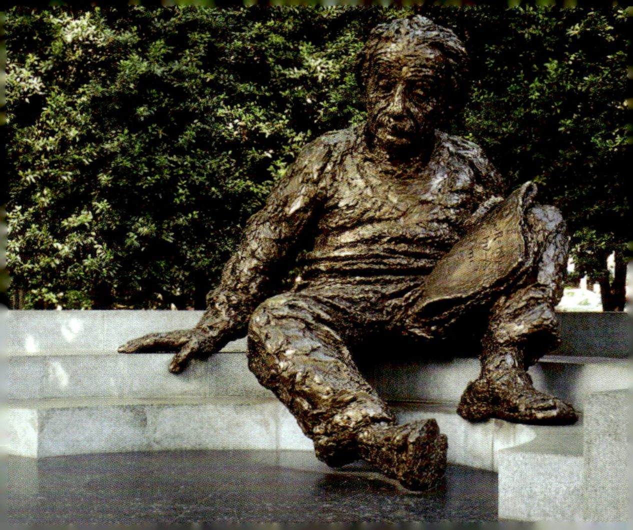

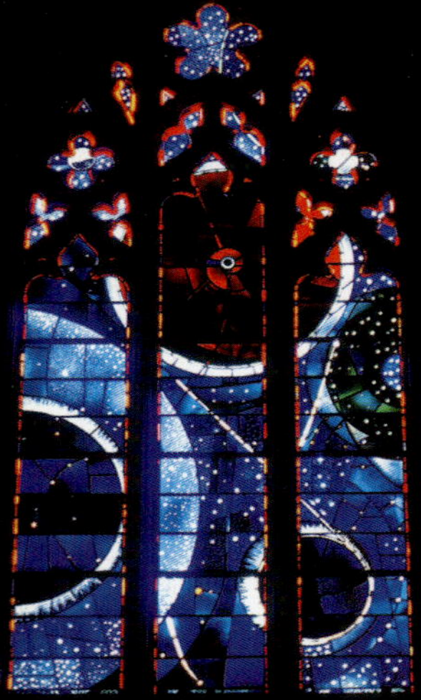

Left *Unofficially called the "Space Window," the Scientists and Technicians Window is one of the more intriguing of Washington National Cathedral's 215 stained glass windows.*

Right *Watergate Complex.*

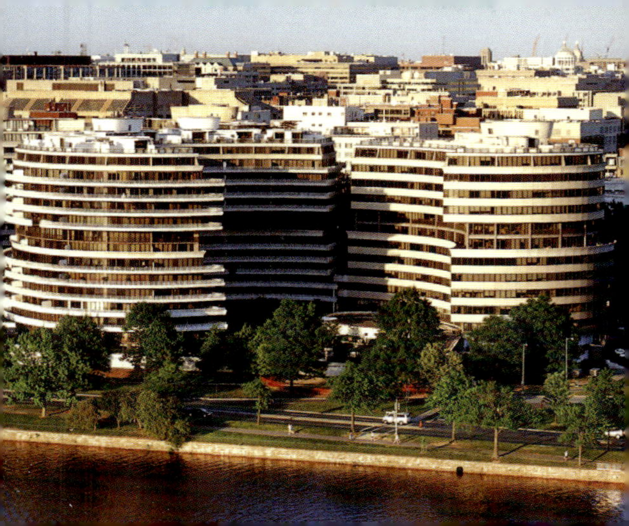

THE WONDERS OF FLIGHT

Opened in 1976, the massive National Air and Space Museum is one of the Smithsonian Institution's most popular museums. With about 200,000 square foot of exhibition space, the collection is a record of the evolution of air and space technology. Among its many life-sized exhibits, most of which were actually flown, are the famous wood, steel, and fabric Flyer built by the Wright brothers (top left), World War II fighter planes, including a Macchi C.202 Folgore and the famed P-51D Mustang (bottom left).

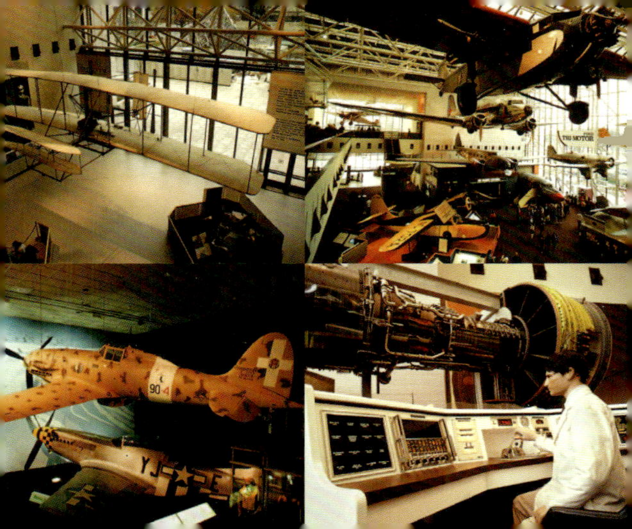
90-4

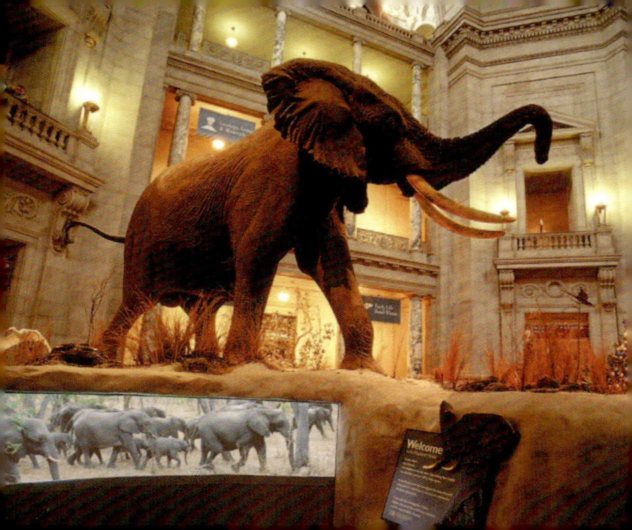
Welcome

African Elephant, National Museum of Natural History

Visitors entering the National Museum of Natural History through the Mall entrance find themselves standing in an eight-sided Rotunda dominated by a magnificent African elephant. At thirteen feet and two inches tall, this awe-inspiring giant cleared the arch of the museum's Rotunda with just an inch to spare when it was moved into place in 1959. Since then, the elephant has become one of the museum's most beloved and enduring symbols.

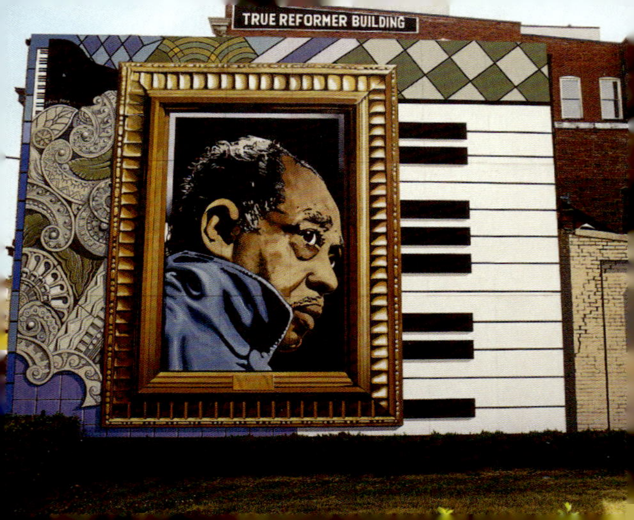
TRUE REFORMER BUILDING

Duke Ellington Mural, Shaw Neighborhood

One of Washington, D.C.'s favorite sons, Edward Kennedy "Duke" Ellington was a dominant figure on the American musical landscape. Born in 1899 and raised in the Shaw neighborhood, Ellington had more than 6,000 works to his credit, including *Don't Get Around Much Anymore*, *Sophisticated Lady*, and *Mood Indigo*. He learned to play piano at a young age, and by the time he was fifteen he was composing his own works. He later moved to New York City where he formed the Duke Ellington Orchestra.

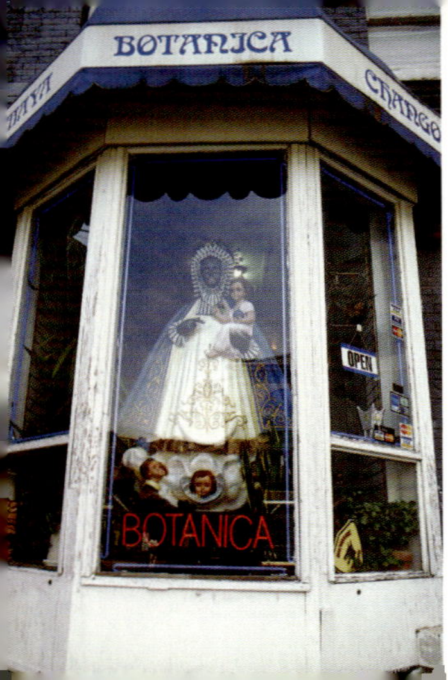

Yemaya Y Chango Botanica *Located in Adams Morgan, the shop sells traditional herbal cures and remedies, alongside the religious paraphernalia associated with the practice of Santeria, a blend of the faith of the people of southern Nigeria, Senegal, and the Guinea coast, and Roman Catholicism.*

House of Prayer

Founded in 1919 in the town of Wareham, Massachusetts, by Pentecostal preacher, Charles Manuel Grace, the United House of Prayer for all People is one of Washington, D.C.'s most active, community-oriented African-American churches featuring extensive music.

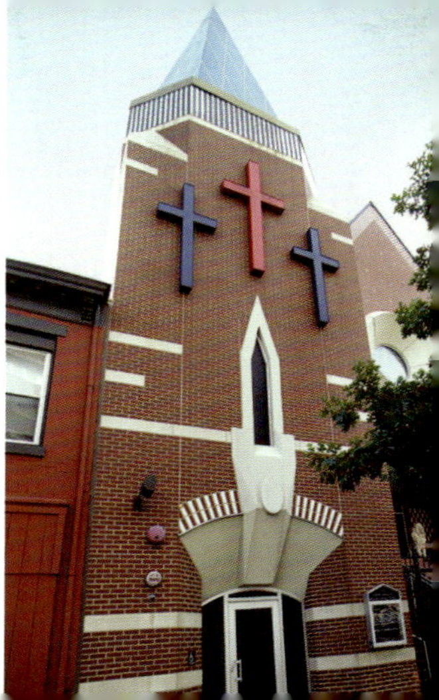

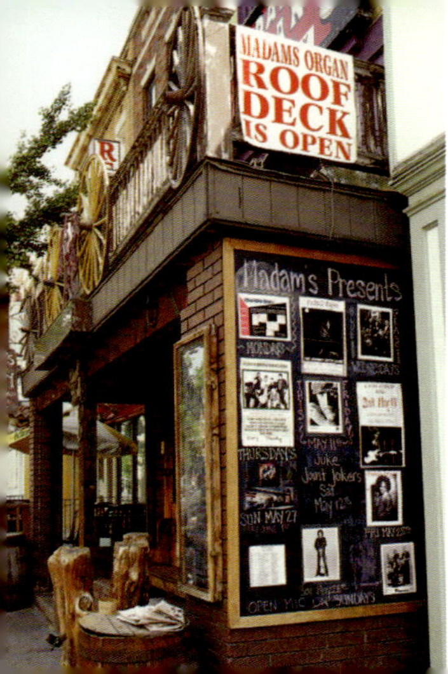

Madam's Organ *The famous Madam's Organ has been offering patrons everything from blues to bluegrass ever since it first opened its doors in Adams Morgan in 1992. This easy-going, eclectic establishment – dubbed "the Heart and Soul of Adams Morgan" – attracts a wide mix of music lovers.*

Roosevelt Island

President Theodore Roosevelt, one of America's most colorful and influential leaders, is memorialized in a seventeen-foot bronze statue located at the center of Roosevelt Island in the Potomac River.

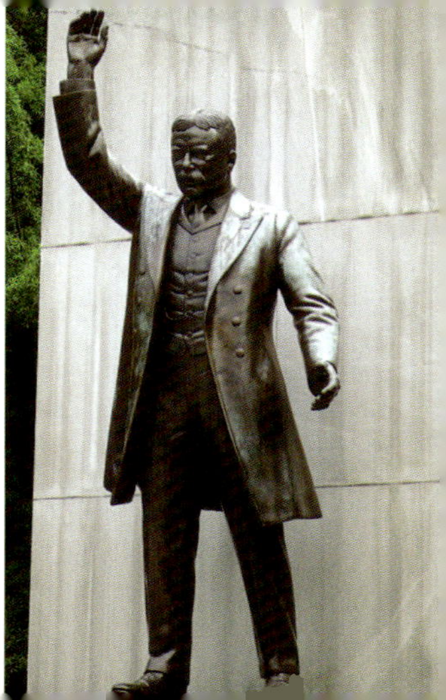

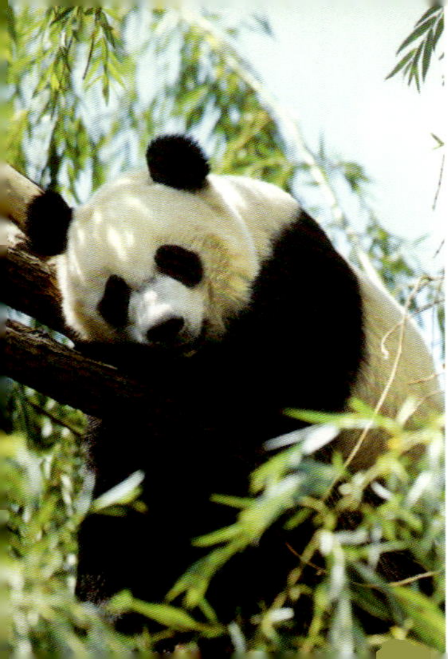

Left *Giant panda, National Zoological Park.*
Right The Breadline, *a life-sized depiction of five men standing in line, waiting for food, is one of sculptor George Segal's poignant portrayals of life during the Great Depression.*

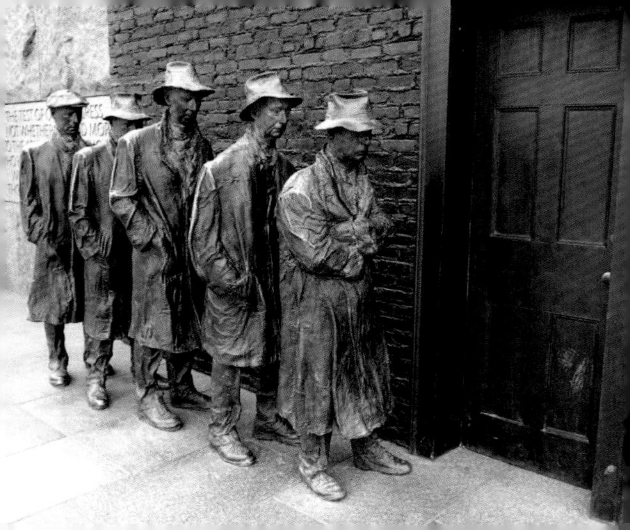

The Pentagon

Home to the Department of Defense, the Pentagon is probably the most well-known symbol of American military strength. Construction of the five-sided building began in September 1941, and proceeded round the clock until its completion a record sixteen months later in January 1943. Today, the Pentagon is the world's largest office building, with more than seventeen miles of corridors and three times the floor space of the Empire State Building.

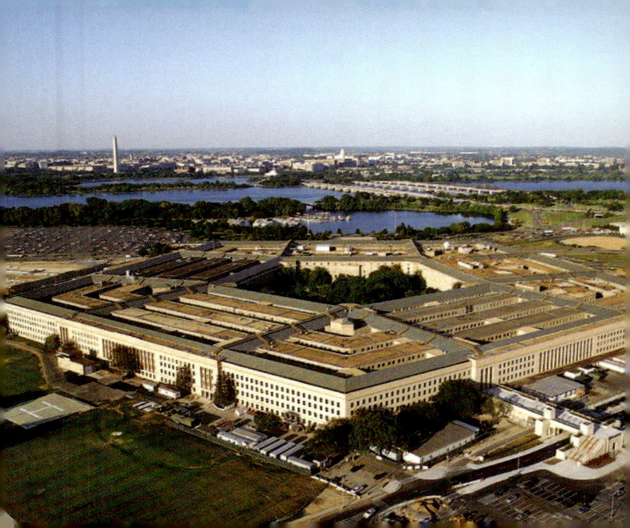

ARLINGTON NATIONAL CEMETERY

The grounds of what is now Arlington National Cemetery were once the home of Confederate General Robert E. Lee. The Lee family were forced to leave their home in May 1861, at the start of the Civil War. Shortly thereafter, in 1864, at the suggestion of General Montgomery Meigs, the government began using the land around Arlington House as a burial ground for Union soldiers. Interestingly, both General Meigs and his son, John, are buried at Arlington.

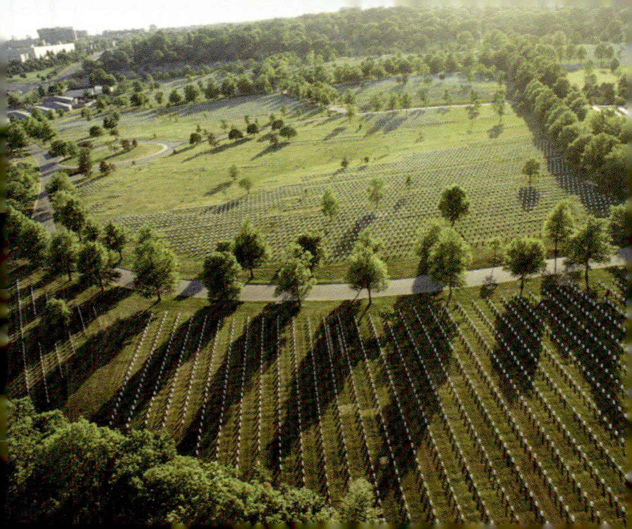

United States Marine Corps War Memorial

Also known as the Iwo Jima Memorial, this monument is dedicated to the thousands of Marines who lost their lives defending the United States and the principles of freedom throughout the world. The sculpture by Felix de Weldon was inspired by a Pulitzer Prize-winning photograph taken by Associated Press photographer Joe Rosenthal during the battle for Iwo Jima, a tiny island 600 miles south of Tokyo, at the height of World War II.

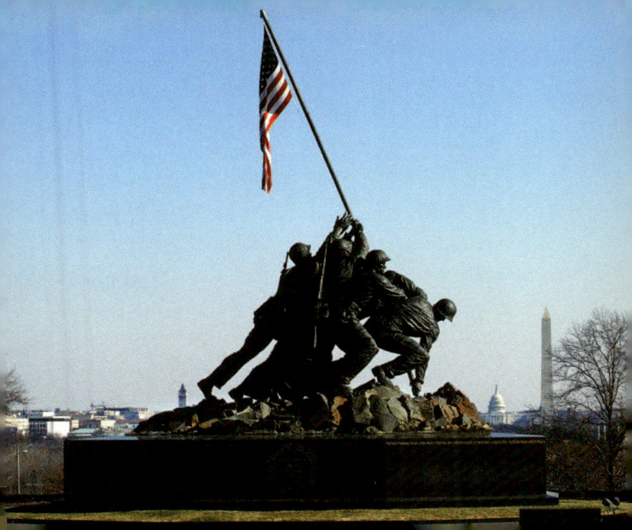

Grave of President John F. Kennedy

An eternal flame marks the graves of President John F. Kennedy, his wife Jacqueline Kennedy Onassis, and two of their infant children. John F. Kennedy's resting place is the most visited grave at Arlington National Cemetery. This site, at the foot of the hill below Arlington House, was selected by Jackie Kennedy after her husband's assassination in 1963. She chose the site because the president had often visited Arlington House to admire the view of Washington, D.C. from across the Potomac River.

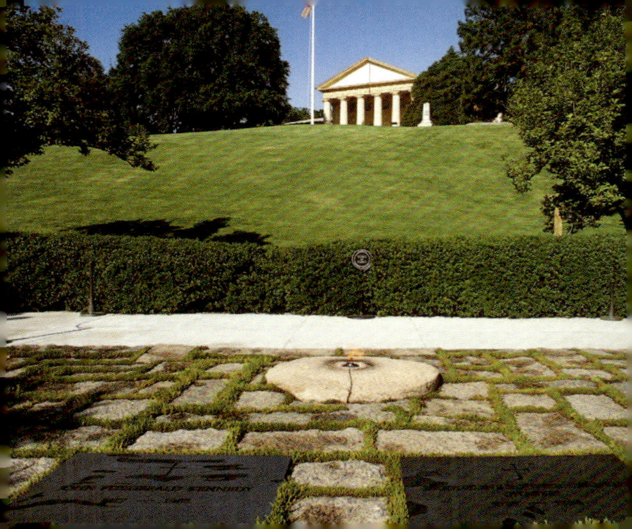

Standing Guard at the Tomb of the Unknowns

Since 1937 the remains of the unidentified servicemen buried in the Tomb of the Unknowns have been under the perpetual watch of an honor guard. The young men and women who volunteer for this duty undergo rigorous training and must work constantly to improve their proficiency.

Overleaf *A Sunday afternoon in spring.*

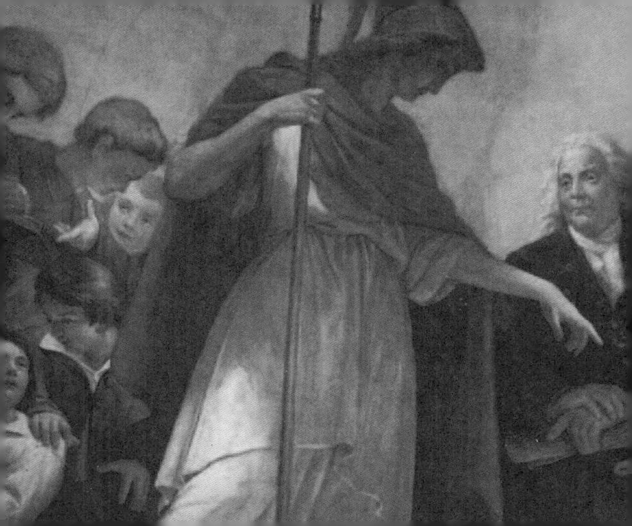

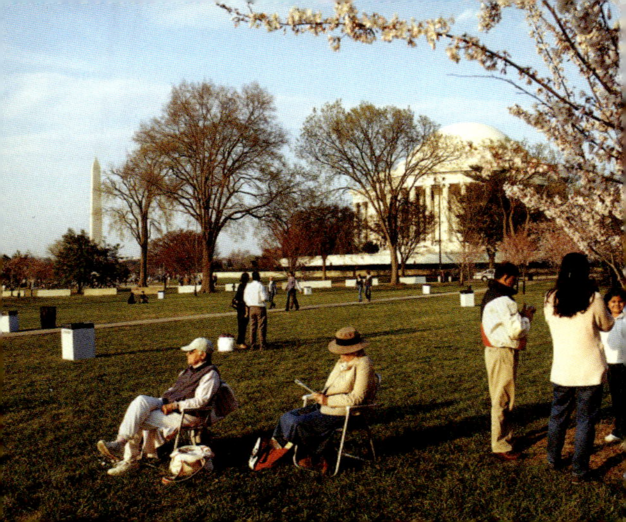

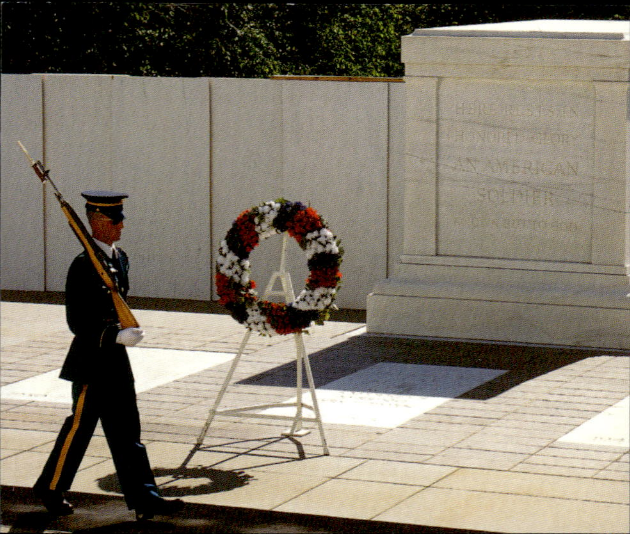
AN AMERICAN
SOLDIER